ME TO WE - THE POWER OF INCLUSION

A HANDBOOK ON INCLUSIVE EDUCATION AT SECONDARY STAGE

DR MEENAKSHI NARULA

"Inclusion is the way to go,

To make sure everyone can grow,

To give each one a chance to shine,

And be a part of life's design.

No one should feel left behind,

Or have to struggle, alone, to find

Their place in this world we share,

Or feel like they don't belong there.

Inclusion means we all have worth,

No matter who we are at birth,

No matter how we look or speak,

We all have the right to seek

A life that's full of love and light,

Where everyone is treated right,

Where differences are celebrated,

And all are welcomed, appreciated.

Inclusion is the key to peace,

To make our troubled world increase

In kindness, empathy, and care,

To build a future that is fair.

So let us embrace inclusion,

And make it our new resolution,

To build a world that's just and true,

Where everyone can be included too."

-Unknown

Contents

Contents

Preface

Dr Meenakshi Narula

As an educator, I have always been passionate about creating an inclusive learning environment that supports the unique needs of all students. However, over the years, I have come to realize that this is not just a personal goal, but a societal imperative. Inclusion is not just a buzzword; it is a fundamental human right that must be upheld in all aspects of our lives.

In this book, **"Me 2 We: Unlocking the Power of Inclusion,"** I have compiled practical strategies and tools for educators to promote inclusion, equity, and social justice in the classroom.

The concept of "Me 2 We" reflects my belief that inclusion is not just about accommodating individual differences; it is about creating a sense of belonging and community for all students. By shifting our focus from "me" to "we," we can build a culture of empathy, collaboration, and mutual respect that supports the growth and development of every learner.

This book is intended for M.Ed. students for their course curriculum with the objective of inspiring them to create a more inclusive and equitable society.

Together, we can unlock the power of inclusion to build a better future for all learners.

Meenakshi Narula

CHAPTER ONE

Inclusive Education

Inclusive education is a concept that promotes the idea that all learners, regardless of their backgrounds, abilities, or disabilities, should have equal access to education and should be fully included in all aspects of school life. Inclusive education values diversity promotes equity and recognizes that every learner has unique strengths and needs that must be accommodated to ensure their success.

Inclusive education is based on the belief that every student has the right to learn in a safe and supportive environment that fosters their academic, social, and emotional development. It involves creating an environment that values and celebrates differences, and that supports the learning needs of all students, including those with disabilities, those from marginalized communities, and those who may be struggling academically.

To create an inclusive education system, educators must adopt a flexible, collaborative, and student-centered approach to teaching and learning. They must be committed to meeting the needs of all students, regardless of their abilities or backgrounds, and must be willing to adapt their instruction to accommodate diverse learning styles and needs.

The goal of inclusive education is to provide every student with the support they need to thrive and succeed, and to ensure that every student has the opportunity to reach their full potential. This approach recognizes that every student is unique, with their own strengths and challenges, and that no one-size-fits-all solution can work for everyone. Inclusive education embraces the differences that exist among students and seeks to leverage those differences as a source of strength and innovation.

Here are some examples of inclusive education in action:

Providing accommodations and support: In an inclusive classroom, students with disabilities receive the accommodations and support they need to participate fully in the learning process. For example, a student with a visual impairment might use braille or audiobooks, while a student with a hearing impairment might use a sign language interpreter.

Differentiating instruction: Inclusive education recognizes that students have different learning styles and abilities. Teachers may use a variety of teaching strategies and materials to differentiate instruction and meet the needs of every student in the classroom. This might include visual aids, hands-on activities, or group projects.

Peer tutoring and mentoring: Inclusive education recognizes that students can learn from each other. Teachers might encourage peer tutoring and mentoring, where students with stronger skills in a particular area help those who are struggling. This approach fosters a sense of community and support among students.

Culturally responsive teaching: Inclusive education values diversity and promotes cultural responsiveness. Teachers may incorporate materials and teaching strategies that reflect the cultural backgrounds and experiences of their students, and create an environment where students feel safe and respected.

Universal design for learning: Inclusive education embraces the principle of universal design for learning, which seeks to create learning environments and materials that are accessible to all students. This might involve using technology or multimedia resources to accommodate different learning styles, or providing multiple ways for students to demonstrate their understanding of a topic.

Overall, inclusive education is about creating a learning environment that is welcoming, supportive, and accessible to all students, regardless of their differences. It recognizes that every student has something valuable to contribute and that by embracing diversity, we can create a more inclusive and equitable society.

CHAPTER TWO

Social Context of Inclusion

Inclusion is a social concept that is deeply embedded in the larger social context. The social context of inclusion includes the cultural, economic, political, and historical factors that shape our understanding of diversity and influence our attitudes and behaviors toward inclusion.

Cultural factors play an important role in shaping our attitudes toward inclusion. Different cultures may have different views on diversity and inclusion and may place different values on different aspects of diversity. For example, in some cultures, disability may be viewed as a sign of weakness, while in others it may be seen as a natural part of the human experience.

Economic factors can also impact inclusion. Socioeconomic status can influence a student's access to resources and opportunities and can impact their ability to participate fully in the educational system. Students from lower-income families may face greater challenges in accessing the resources and support they need to succeed in school.

Political factors can also shape our understanding of inclusion. Laws and policies that promote inclusion and equity can create a supportive environment for students from diverse backgrounds. On the other hand, policies that discriminate against certain groups can create barriers to inclusion and perpetuate inequalities.

Historical factors also play a role in shaping our understanding of inclusion. Historical injustices, such as discrimination and segregation, can have long-lasting effects on certain groups of students. These effects can be passed down from one generation to the next, perpetuating inequalities and creating new barriers to inclusion.

Overall, the social context of inclusion is complex and multifaceted. It involves a wide range of cultural, economic, political, and historical factors that shape our attitudes and behaviors towards inclusion. By understanding these factors, we can create a more inclusive and equitable educational system that values diversity and promotes the success of all students.

CHAPTER THREE

Psychological Context of Inclusion

The psychological context of inclusion refers to the individual and interpersonal factors that impact inclusion, including the attitudes, beliefs, and behaviors of students, teachers, and other members of the educational community. The psychological context of inclusion is important because it can either facilitate or hinder the process of inclusion.

One important psychological factor that impacts inclusion is attitudes toward diversity. Positive attitudes towards diversity and inclusion can help create a welcoming and supportive environment for all students. On the other hand, negative attitudes toward diversity can lead to discrimination, bullying, and exclusion.

Another important factor is self-efficacy or the belief in one's ability to succeed in a particular task or situation. Students who believe in their ability to learn and succeed are more likely to participate fully in the educational system and feel included in the classroom. Teachers who have a strong sense of self-efficacy are more likely to be effective in promoting inclusion and helping all students succeed.

The social identity theory suggests that individuals derive their sense of self from the groups they belong to. This theory is relevant to inclusion because it explains how group membership can impact behavior and attitudes toward others. Students who feel a strong sense of belonging in a particular group are more likely to be accepting of others who are different from them.

In addition, interpersonal factors such as communication, collaboration, and empathy play a role in creating a supportive and inclusive learning environment. Teachers who are skilled in communicating with students from diverse backgrounds, collaborating with other teachers and professionals, and demonstrating empathy towards their students are more likely to create a positive learning environment that promotes inclusion.

Overall, the psychological context of inclusion is complex and multifaceted and includes a wide range of individual and interpersonal factors that impact inclusion. By understanding these factors and promoting positive attitudes, beliefs, and behaviors, we can create a more inclusive and supportive learning environment for all students.

CHAPTER FOUR

Educational Context of Inclusion

The educational context of inclusion refers to the policies, practices, and structures that promote the inclusion of all students in the educational system.

Here are some examples of the educational context of inclusion:

Universal design for learning (UDL): UDL is an approach to teaching that involves designing instruction to meet the needs of all students, regardless of their backgrounds or abilities. UDL includes strategies such as providing multiple means of representation, action and expression, and engagement, which allows students to access and participate in learning in ways that work best for them.

Individualized Education Program (IEP): An IEP is a legal document that outlines the individualized educational goals and accommodations for a student with a disability. IEPs are designed to help students with disabilities access the curriculum and participate fully in the educational system.

Co-teaching: Co-teaching involves two or more teachers working together in the same classroom to support all students. This approach can help meet the needs of students with diverse backgrounds and abilities, and promote inclusion by creating a supportive and collaborative learning environment.

Culturally responsive teaching: Culturally responsive teaching involves recognizing and valuing the diverse cultural backgrounds of students and using this knowledge to inform instructional practices. This approach can help create a more inclusive learning environment by promoting cultural understanding and respect among students and teachers.

Multi-tiered system of support (MTSS): MTSS is an approach to providing support for students with diverse learning needs. It involves providing a range of supports and interventions, including academic and behavioral supports, based on the individual needs of each student. MTSS can help ensure that all students have access to the resources and support they need to succeed in school.

Overall, the educational context of inclusion involves creating a supportive and inclusive learning environment that meets the needs of all students, regardless of their backgrounds or abilities. By implementing policies, practices, and structures that promote inclusion, educators can help ensure that all students have the opportunity to learn and succeed in school.

CHAPTER FIVE

National Policy Statements on Inclusion

In India, there are several policy statements and initiatives that promote inclusion in education.

Here are some examples:

1. The Right of Children to Free and Compulsory Education (RTE) Act, 2009: This act ensures that all children between the ages of 6 and 14 have the right to free and compulsory education. The act also promotes inclusion by requiring that all schools provide admission to children with disabilities, and by prohibiting discrimination based on gender, caste, religion, or disability.

2. Sarva Shiksha Abhiyan (SSA): This is a flagship program of the Indian government that aims to provide universal elementary education to all children. The program includes several initiatives that promote inclusion, such as the creation of special training programs for teachers to work with children with disabilities, and the provision of assistive devices and technology to support their learning.

3. Inclusive Education for Disabled at Secondary Stage (IEDSS): This is a scheme launched by the government of India to support the education of students with disabilities in secondary schools. The scheme provides financial assistance to schools to support the education of children with disabilities, and includes provisions for teacher training and the provision of assistive devices and technology.

4. National Curriculum Framework (NCF), 2005: The NCF is a policy statement that provides guidelines for the development of a national curriculum. The framework emphasizes the importance of inclusiveness in education and calls for the development of a curriculum that is sensitive to the needs of all learners.

5. The Draft National Education Policy (NEP), 2019: The draft NEP includes several initiatives that promote inclusion, such as the establishment of a National Education Technology Forum to support the use of technology in education, and the development of a National Sign Language Mission to support the education of students who are deaf or hard of hearing.

NEP 2020 and Inclusive Education

The National Education Policy (NEP) 2020 is a comprehensive policy document released by the Government of India that lays out a vision for the future of education in India. The policy places a strong emphasis on inclusive education and includes several initiatives to promote inclusion. Here are some key features of the NEP 2020 related to inclusive education:

1. Early Childhood Care and Education (ECCE): The policy recognizes the importance of early childhood education and care in promoting inclusion. It calls for the establishment of ECCE centers in every anganwadi (village childcare center) and for the integration of ECCE with primary education.

2. Special Education: The NEP 2020 recognizes the need for a more comprehensive approach to special education that goes beyond the traditional focus on disability. The policy calls for the establishment of resource centers to support students with special needs, and for the inclusion of sign language and braille as languages of instruction in schools.

3. Multilingualism: The NEP 2020 emphasizes the importance of multilingualism in promoting inclusion and calls for the development of multilingual educational materials. The policy also calls for the use of the home language or mother tongue as the medium of instruction in primary education.

4. Universal Access: The NEP 2020 calls for the provision of equitable access to education for all students, regardless of their socio-economic background, gender, or religion. The policy emphasizes the importance of reducing drop-out rates and improving retention rates, especially among marginalized groups.

5. Teacher Education: The NEP 2020 recognizes the importance of teacher education in promoting inclusion and calls for the development of a comprehensive teacher education program. The policy emphasizes the need for teacher training in areas such as special education, multilingualism, and inclusive pedagogy.

The NEP 2020 places a strong emphasis on inclusive education and includes several initiatives to promote inclusion in the Indian education system. The policy recognizes the importance of early childhood education, special education, multilingualism, and equitable access to education, and calls for the development of a comprehensive teacher education program. These initiatives are aimed at creating a more inclusive and equitable education system that meets the needs of all learners, regardless of their backgrounds or abilities.

Overall, India has several policy statements and initiatives that promote inclusion in education. These initiatives are aimed at creating a more inclusive and equitable educational system that meets the needs of all learners, regardless of their backgrounds or abilities.

CHAPTER SIX

International Policy Statements on Inclusion

There are several international policies that promote inclusion in education.

Here are some examples:

1. United Nations Convention on the Rights of Persons with Disabilities (UNCRPD): This convention, adopted in 2006, recognizes the rights of persons with disabilities, including the right to education without discrimination, and calls for the provision of reasonable accommodations and support.

2. Sustainable Development Goals (SDGs): Goal 4 of the SDGs calls for the provision of inclusive and equitable quality education and the promotion of lifelong learning opportunities for all.

3. Education for All (EFA): Launched by UNESCO in 2000, the EFA initiative aimed to provide quality education for all by 2015, and included several goals related to inclusion.

4. Salamanca Statement and Framework for Action on Special Needs Education: This statement, adopted in 1994, promotes inclusive education as a means of promoting the right to education for all children, regardless of their abilities.

5. The Convention on the Rights of the Child (CRC): This convention, adopted in 1989, recognizes the importance of inclusive education and calls for the provision of education to all children, without discrimination.

6. World Declaration on Education for All: Adopted in 1990, this declaration promotes the provision of education for all, with a particular focus on disadvantaged and marginalized groups.

7. United Nations Universal Declaration of Human Rights (UDHR): This declaration, adopted in 1948, recognizes the right to education as a fundamental human right.

8. **The International Covenant on Economic, Social and Cultural Rights (ICESCR):** This covenant, adopted in 1966, recognizes the right to education as a fundamental human right and calls for the provision of equal access to education.

9. **The Millennium Development Goals (MDGs):** The MDGs, adopted in 2000, included a goal to achieve universal primary education and promote gender equality in education.

10. **Incheon Declaration and Framework for Action for the Implementation of Sustainable Development Goal 4:** This declaration, adopted in 2015, provides guidance on the implementation of Goal 4 of the SDGs, including the promotion of inclusive education.

CHAPTER SEVEN

Indian Govt. Initiatives to Promote Inclusion in Education

The Indian government has launched several initiatives to promote inclusion in education.

Here are ten such initiatives:

1. Sarva Shiksha Abhiyan (SSA): Launched in 2001, SSA aims to provide universal access to primary education, with a focus on marginalized groups, such as girls, children from disadvantaged backgrounds, and children with disabilities.

2. Inclusive Education for Disabled at Secondary Stage (IEDSS): Launched in 2009, IEDSS aims to provide support for the education of children with disabilities in mainstream secondary schools.

3. Rashtriya Madhyamik Shiksha Abhiyan (RMSA): Launched in 2009, RMSA aims to provide access to secondary education for all children, with a focus on marginalized groups.

4. Samagra Shiksha Abhiyan (SSA): Launched in 2018, SSA aims to provide equitable and inclusive education for all children, with a focus on improving learning outcomes and reducing disparities.

5. National Scheme of Incentive to Girls for Secondary Education (NSIGSE): Launched in 2008, NSIGSE provides incentives for the education of girls from disadvantaged backgrounds, with a focus on secondary education.

6. Mid-Day Meal Scheme (MDMS): Launched in 1995, MDMS provides free, nutritious meals to children in government schools, with a focus on improving attendance and reducing malnutrition.

7. Kasturba Gandhi Balika Vidyalaya (KGBV): Launched in 2004, KGBV provides residential schools for girls from disadvantaged backgrounds, with a focus on improving access to education and reducing gender disparities.

8. National Programme for Education of Girls at Elementary Level (NPEGEL): Launched in 2003, NPEGEL aims to improve the access and quality of education for girls from disadvantaged backgrounds.

9. National Scholarship Scheme (NSS): Launched in 2017, NSS provides scholarships for students from disadvantaged backgrounds, including those with disabilities, to enable them to continue their education.

10. Scheme for Providing Quality Education in Madrasas (SPQEM): Launched in 2009, SPQEM aims to provide quality education to students in madrasas, with a focus on modernizing the curriculum and improving learning outcomes.

CHAPTER EIGHT

The Mental Health Act, 1987

The Mental Health Act of 1987 is a law in India that provides for the treatment and care of people with mental illness. The act is intended to safeguard the rights of people with mental illness, protect them from abuse and neglect, and ensure that they receive appropriate treatment and care.

Here are 10 key provisions of the Mental Health Act of 1987 in India:

1. **Definition of mental illness:** The act defines mental illness as any disorder of the mind that affects a person's thought processes, mood, or behavior.
2. **Establishment of mental health authorities:** The act provides for the establishment of central and state mental health authorities to oversee the implementation of the act and ensure the provision of mental health services.
3. **Admission, treatment, and discharge:** The act provides for both voluntary and involuntary admission of people with mental illness to mental health establishments, as well as their treatment and discharge.
4. **Guardianship:** The act allows for the appointment of guardians for people with mental illness who are unable to make decisions for themselves.
5. **Rights of persons with mental illness:** The act provides for several rights of persons with mental illness, including the right to humane treatment and care, access to medical records, and confidentiality.
6. **Prohibition of cruel, inhuman, and degrading treatment:** The act prohibits the use of cruel, inhuman, and degrading treatment or punishment on people with mental illness.
7. **Establishment of mental health review boards:** The act provides for the establishment of mental health review boards to review the cases of people with mental illness who are involuntarily admitted to mental

health establishments.

8. **Community-based mental health services:** The 2018 amendment to the act introduced the provision for the establishment of community-based mental health services.

9. **Decriminalization of suicide:** The 2018 amendment also decriminalized suicide, recognizing it as a mental health issue rather than a criminal offense.

10. **Rights of caregivers:** The act recognizes the rights of caregivers, including the right to participate in the treatment of a person with mental illness and to be informed about their condition and treatment.

CHAPTER NINE

Rehabiliation Council of India Act, 1992

The Rehabilitation Council of India Act is a law enacted by the Indian Parliament in 1992. The purpose of the act is to establish the Rehabilitation Council of India (RCI) as a statutory body for regulating and monitoring the training and education of rehabilitation professionals in India.

The key provisions of the Rehabilitation Council of India Act include:

1. **Establishment of the Rehabilitation Council of India:** The act establishes the Rehabilitation Council of India as a statutory body to regulate and monitor the training and education of rehabilitation professionals in India.

2. **Composition of the Council:** The act provides for the composition of the Council, which includes a Chairman and members appointed by the Central Government, as well as representatives from various stakeholder groups, such as rehabilitation professionals, organizations representing persons with disabilities, and representatives from the Ministry of Health and Family Welfare.

3. **Functions of the Council:** The act sets out the functions of the Council, which include regulating and monitoring the training and education of rehabilitation professionals, setting standards for the training and education of rehabilitation professionals, maintaining a register of qualified professionals, and promoting research in rehabilitation and related fields.

4. **Recognition of Institutions:** The act provides for the recognition of institutions that provide training and education in rehabilitation and related fields, and sets out the criteria that institutions must meet in order to be recognized.

5. **Qualifications for Professionals:** The act sets out the qualifications required for individuals to be registered as rehabilitation professionals, including educational qualifications and experience.
6. **Registration of Professionals:** The act provides for the registration of qualified rehabilitation professionals with the Council, and sets out the procedures for registration.
7. **Professional Standards:** The act sets out the professional standards that registered rehabilitation professionals must adhere to, and provides for the suspension or cancellation of registration for professionals who fail to meet these standards.
8. **Promotion of Research:** The act provides for the promotion of research in rehabilitation and related fields, including the establishment of research centers and the dissemination of research findings.
9. **Funding:** The act provides for the funding of the Rehabilitation Council of India, including the collection of fees from registered professionals and the receipt of grants from the Central Government.
10. **Penalties:** The act provides for penalties for individuals and institutions that violate its provisions, including fines and imprisonment.

CHAPTER TEN

The Persons with Disabilities Act (PWD Act),1995

The Persons with Disabilities Act (PWD Act) 1995 is a law enacted by the Indian Parliament to provide for the protection of rights and full participation of persons with disabilities in society. The PWD Act defines a person with disability as someone who has one or more of the following impairments: blindness, low vision, leprosy-cured, hearing impairment, locomotor disability, mental retardation or mental illness.

The key provisions of the Persons with Disabilities Act 1995 include:

1. **Definition of disability:** The act defines disability and lists out the various disabilities that are covered under the act.
2. **Non-discrimination:** The act prohibits discrimination against persons with disabilities in various areas, including employment, education, and access to public facilities.
3. **Reservation:** The act provides for reservation of seats in educational institutions and in government jobs for persons with disabilities.
4. **Accessible environment:** The act requires public buildings, roads, transport, and other facilities to be made accessible for persons with disabilities.
5. **Identification and assessment of disabilities:** The act provides for the identification and assessment of disabilities, and for the issuance of disability certificates.
6. **Guardianship:** The act provides for the appointment of guardians for persons with disabilities who are unable to take care of themselves.
7. **Establishment of National Fund:** The act provides for the establishment of a National Fund for Persons with Disabilities for the promotion of welfare measures, research and development, and other purposes.

8. **Implementation:** The act provides for the establishment of State and Central Coordination Committees for the implementation of the provisions of the act.

9. **Penalties:** The act provides for penalties for violations of its provisions, including fines and imprisonment.

The Persons with Disabilities Act 1995 is an important law in India that seeks to ensure the rights and full participation of persons with disabilities in society. The act provides a framework for the protection of the rights of persons with disabilities and for the promotion of their welfare and inclusion in all areas of life.

CHAPTER ELEVEN

The National Trust for Welfare of Persons with Autism, Cerebral Palsy, Mental Retardation and Multiple Disabilities Act, 1999

The National Trust for Welfare of Persons with Autism, Cerebral Palsy, Mental Retardation, and Multiple Disabilities Act 1999 is an important law enacted by the Indian Parliament to provide for the welfare of persons with disabilities. The act aims to enable and empower persons with disabilities to live as independently and as fully as possible in society.

The key provisions of the National Trust for Welfare of Persons with Autism, Cerebral Palsy, Mental Retardation, and Multiple Disabilities Act 1999 include:

1. **Definition of disability:** The act defines disability and lists out the various disabilities that are covered under the act, including autism, cerebral palsy, mental retardation, and multiple disabilities.
2. **Establishment of National Trust:** The act provides for the establishment of the National Trust for Welfare of Persons with Autism, Cerebral Palsy, Mental Retardation, and Multiple Disabilities to enable persons with disabilities to live as independently and as fully as possible in society.
3. **Registration of Organizations:** The act provides for the registration of organizations working for the welfare of persons with disabilities, and

sets out the procedures for registration.

4. **Functions of the National Trust:** The act sets out the functions of the National Trust, which include promoting research in the field of disabilities, developing and implementing programs for the welfare of persons with disabilities, and providing support to registered organizations working for the welfare of persons with disabilities.

5. **Grants and Funding:** The act provides for the provision of grants and funding to registered organizations working for the welfare of persons with disabilities.

6. **Protection of Rights:** The act provides for the protection of the rights of persons with disabilities, including their right to dignity, equality, and non-discrimination.

7. **Appointment of Guardians:** The act provides for the appointment of guardians for persons with disabilities who are unable to take care of themselves.

8. **Implementation:** The act provides for the establishment of State and Central Coordination Committees for the implementation of the provisions of the act.

9. **Penalties:** The act provides penalties for violations of its provisions, including fines and imprisonment.

The National Trust for Welfare of Persons with Autism, Cerebral Palsy, Mental Retardation and Multiple Disabilities Act 1999 is an important law in India that seeks to promote the welfare and inclusion of persons with disabilities in society. The act provides a framework for the protection of the rights of persons with disabilities and for the promotion of their independence and well-being.

CHAPTER TWELVE

Issues in Planning and Management of Education of Children and Persons with Disabilities

1. **Access:** One of the main issues in planning and managing education for children and persons with disabilities is ensuring that they have access to education, including physical access to schools and educational materials.

2. **Inclusive Education:** Providing inclusive education that meets the needs of all learners, regardless of their disability or special needs, can be challenging.

3. **Training of Teachers:** Training teachers to effectively teach and manage students with disabilities can be difficult, particularly in rural or remote areas.

4. **Quality Education:** Ensuring that children and persons with disabilities receive quality education that is on par with that provided to non-disabled students is a challenge.

5. **Infrastructure:** Providing the necessary infrastructure, such as ramps, accessible toilets, and assistive devices, is essential but can be costly.

6. **Resource Allocation:** Allocating resources and funding for inclusive education programs can be challenging, particularly in low-income countries.

7. **Advocacy:** Advocating for the rights of children and persons with disabilities to education and other basic human rights is necessary to

ensure they receive the support they need.

8. **Attitudes and Stereotypes:** Overcoming negative attitudes and stereotypes towards children and persons with disabilities is important in ensuring their inclusion in education.

9. **Early Identification:** Early identification and intervention of disabilities is crucial for successful educational outcomes, but can be challenging in areas without access to healthcare services.

10. **Policy and Legal Frameworks:** Ensuring that national policies and legal frameworks promote inclusive education for children and persons with disabilities is essential.

11. **Coordination:** Effective coordination between different stakeholders, including educators, policymakers, and disability rights organizations, is important to ensure that inclusive education programs are successful.

12. **Participation:** Involving children and persons with disabilities and their families in the planning and management of inclusive education programs is important to ensure their needs are met.

13. **Research:** Conducting research on effective teaching and management practices for students with disabilities can help improve the quality of education provided.

14. **Evaluation:** Evaluating the effectiveness of inclusive education programs is important to identify areas for improvement and ensure that children and persons with disabilities receive the support they need.

15. **Sustainability:** Ensuring the sustainability of inclusive education programs over the long term is important to ensure that children and persons with disabilities receive the support they need to reach their full potential.

Issues in Identification of Special Education Needs

Identifying special education needs can be challenging due to various issues such as:

1. **Lack of Awareness:** Parents, teachers, and other professionals may lack awareness of the signs and symptoms of specific disabilities or special needs, making it difficult to identify children who may require special education.
2. **Stigma and Stereotypes:** There may be a stigma associated with disabilities, leading to negative attitudes and stereotypes that can prevent children from receiving the support they need.
3. **Language Barriers:** Language barriers may prevent some children from receiving appropriate assessments or support, particularly in areas with diverse linguistic communities.
4. **Cultural Differences:** Cultural differences can affect the way that disabilities and special needs are perceived and understood, making it difficult to identify children who may require special education.
5. **Lack of Access to Services:** Children living in remote or rural areas may not have access to the necessary services and support to identify and address their special education needs.
6. **Limited Assessment Tools:** Limited assessment tools or assessments that are not culturally appropriate or language-specific can lead to inaccurate identification of special education needs.
7. **Co-morbidity:** Some children may have multiple disabilities or conditions, making it difficult to identify and provide appropriate support for each individual need.

8. **Late Identification:** Some children may not be identified as having special education needs until they have already experienced significant challenges in their education, leading to delays in receiving support.

9. **Lack of Coordination:** Lack of coordination between different professionals, including educators, healthcare providers, and parents, can make it difficult to identify special education needs and provide appropriate support.

10. **Financial Constraints:** The cost of assessments and support services may be a barrier to identifying and addressing special education needs, particularly in low-income areas.

CHAPTER FOURTEEN

Issues in Assessment of Special Education Needs

Assessment is an essential component of planning and managing special education needs.

Some assessment issues that can arise in this context include:

1. **Assessment Tools:** Limited assessment tools or assessments that are not culturally appropriate or language-specific can lead to inaccurate identification of special education needs.
2. **Validity and Reliability:** The validity and reliability of assessment tools used to identify special education needs can be a concern, particularly if they are not regularly updated or tested.
3. **Bias:** The potential for bias in the assessment process, including cultural or linguistic bias, can lead to inaccurate identification of special education needs.
4. **Timing:** The timing of assessments can be critical to identifying special education needs, and delays in assessment can result in delays in receiving appropriate support.
5. **Coordination:** Coordination between different professionals involved in the assessment process is essential to ensure that assessments are comprehensive and provide a clear understanding of the child's needs.
6. **Accessibility:** Assessment tools and procedures should be accessible to all students, including those with physical or sensory disabilities.
7. **Informed Consent:** Informed consent from parents or guardians is necessary before conducting any assessments or evaluations.
8. **Language Barriers:** Language barriers may prevent some children from receiving appropriate assessments or support, particularly in areas with diverse linguistic communities.

9. **Standardization:** Standardization of assessment tools and procedures can help ensure that all children are assessed using the same criteria, reducing the potential for bias and increasing accuracy.

10. **Multi-Disciplinary Assessment:** Multi-disciplinary assessments involving professionals from different fields, including education, healthcare, and psychology, can provide a more comprehensive understanding of a child's needs and lead to better planning and management of special education needs.

CHAPTER FIFTEEN

Issues in Certification of Special Education Needs

Certification of special education needs is an important aspect of ensuring that children receive appropriate support and services.

Some issues that can arise in the certification process include:

1. **Lack of Standardization:** Lack of standardization in the certification process can lead to inconsistencies in identifying and managing special education needs.
2. **Complexity:** The certification process can be complex and time-consuming, making it difficult for parents and educators to navigate.
3. **Limited Assessment Tools:** Limited assessment tools or assessments that are not culturally appropriate or language-specific can lead to inaccurate identification of special education needs.
4. **Bias:** The potential for bias in the certification process, including cultural or linguistic bias, can lead to inaccurate identification of special education needs.
5. **Lack of Clarity:** Lack of clarity in the certification process, including unclear criteria or requirements, can lead to confusion and delays in identifying and addressing special education needs.
6. **Financial Constraints:** The cost of assessments and support services may be a barrier to obtaining certification, particularly in low-income areas.
7. **Accessibility:** Certification processes should be accessible to all students, including those with physical or sensory disabilities.
8. **Coordination:** Coordination between different professionals involved in the certification process is essential to ensure that assessments are comprehensive and provide a clear understanding of the child's needs.

9. **Time Constraints:** Timelines for certification can be a concern, particularly if delays in the process result in delays in receiving appropriate support.

10. **Multi-Disciplinary Certification:** Multi-disciplinary certification involving professionals from different fields, including education, healthcare, and psychology, can provide a more comprehensive understanding of a child's needs and lead to better planning and management of special education needs.

CHAPTER SIXTEEN

Rights of Children with Disabilities

Children with disabilities have the same rights as other children and are entitled to additional protections and support.

Here are some of the key rights of children with disabilities:

1. **Right to Education:** Children with disabilities have the right to an inclusive education that meets their needs and enables them to achieve their full potential.
2. **Right to Healthcare:** Children with disabilities have the right to accessible, affordable, and appropriate healthcare services, including rehabilitation and assistive technologies.
3. **Right to Protection:** Children with disabilities are entitled to protection from abuse, neglect, and exploitation, including discrimination based on their disability.
4. **Right to Participation:** Children with disabilities have the right to participate fully in all aspects of society, including in decision-making processes that affect them.
5. **Right to Family Life:** Children with disabilities have the right to live with their families or other caregivers, and to receive appropriate support to enable them to do so.
6. **Right to Play:** Children with disabilities have the right to engage in play, recreation, and leisure activities on an equal basis with other children.
7. **Right to Social Protection:** Children with disabilities have the right to social protection, including access to social security, health insurance, and other forms of support.
8. **Right to Non-Discrimination:** Children with disabilities have the right to be protected from discrimination based on their disability, and to enjoy

their rights without discrimination of any kind.

9. **Right to Accessible Information:** Children with disabilities have the right to access information and communication, including in formats that are accessible to them.

10. **Right to Freedom of Expression:** Children with disabilities have the right to express themselves and communicate in ways that are appropriate to their abilities, and to have their views taken into account in all matters affecting them.

CHAPTER SEVENTEEN

Article 23: The Rights of Children with Disabilities

Article 23 of the United Nations Convention on the Rights of Persons with Disabilities (UNCRPD) specifically outlines the rights of children with disabilities.

Some of the key provisions include:

1. **Right to an Inclusive Education:** Children with disabilities have the right to education that is inclusive and enables them to reach their full potential.
2. **Right to Healthcare:** Children with disabilities have the right to accessible, affordable, and appropriate healthcare services, including rehabilitation and assistive technologies.
3. **Right to Protection from Abuse and Neglect:** Children with disabilities have the right to protection from all forms of abuse, neglect, and exploitation.
4. **Right to Family Life:** Children with disabilities have the right to live with their families or other caregivers, and to receive appropriate support to enable them to do so.
5. **Right to Play and Leisure:** Children with disabilities have the right to participate in play, recreation, and leisure activities on an equal basis with other children.
6. **Right to Non-Discrimination:** Children with disabilities have the right to be protected from discrimination based on their disability, and to enjoy their rights without discrimination of any kind.
7. **Right to Accessible Information:** Children with disabilities have the right to access information and communication, including in formats that are accessible to them.

8. **Right to Freedom of Expression:** Children with disabilities have the right to express themselves and communicate in ways that are appropriate to their abilities, and to have their views taken into account in all matters affecting them.
9. **Right to Participation:** Children with disabilities have the right to participate fully in all aspects of society, including in decision-making processes that affect them.
10. **Right to Social Protection:** Children with disabilities have the right to social protection, including access to social security, health insurance, and other forms of support.

The Implications for Inclusive Education

The implications for inclusive education provisions based on the rights of children with disabilities include:

1. **Access to Education:** Inclusive education must be made accessible to all children with disabilities. Schools should provide reasonable accommodations and modifications to enable children with disabilities to participate in all aspects of education.
2. **Qualified Teachers:** Teachers must be trained and qualified to provide inclusive education. They should have knowledge of disability-specific needs, teaching methods, and assistive technologies.
3. **Individualized Education Plan:** Each child with a disability should have an individualized education plan (IEP) that outlines their specific needs, goals, and accommodations.
4. **Accessible Curriculum:** The curriculum should be accessible to all children with disabilities. Materials should be provided in various formats that are accessible to children with different disabilities.
5. **Assistive Technologies:** Assistive technologies should be provided to enable children with disabilities to participate fully in education. Examples include braille machines, hearing aids, and communication devices.
6. **Inclusive Environment:** The school environment should be inclusive and barrier-free. Physical barriers, such as stairs or narrow doorways, should be removed, and the environment should be accessible to all children.

7. **Professional Development:** Teachers and school staff should receive ongoing professional development to improve their knowledge and skills in inclusive education.

8. **Parental Involvement:** Parents of children with disabilities should be involved in the education process, including the development of the child's IEP.

9. **Collaboration:** Collaboration between schools, parents, and disability organizations should be encouraged to ensure that the needs of children with disabilities are met.

10. **Monitoring and Evaluation:** The progress of children with disabilities in inclusive education should be monitored and evaluated regularly to ensure that their needs are being met and adjustments can be made as necessary.

CHAPTER EIGHTEEN

Role of Govt. Organizations in the Implementation of Inclusive Education

Government organizations play a crucial role in ensuring the implementation of inclusive education policies and programs.

Some of the key roles of government organizations in inclusive education include:

1. **Policy Development:** Government organizations are responsible for developing policies and guidelines that promote inclusive education for children with disabilities.
2. **Resource Allocation:** Government organizations allocate resources for the implementation of inclusive education programs and initiatives, such as funding for assistive technologies and teacher training.
3. **Curriculum Development:** Government organizations develop and revise the curriculum to ensure that it is inclusive and accessible to all students, including those with disabilities.
4. **Teacher Training:** Government organizations provide training to teachers and other education professionals to enable them to effectively teach students with disabilities.
5. **Monitoring and Evaluation:** Government organizations monitor and evaluate the implementation of inclusive education policies and programs to ensure that they are effective and meet the needs of all students.
6. **Research:** Government organizations conduct research on inclusive education to inform policy development and improve practice.

7. **Advocacy:** Government organizations advocate for the rights of children with disabilities and promote inclusive education policies and programs.

8. **Collaboration:** Government organizations collaborate with other stakeholders, such as disability organizations and parents, to ensure that the needs of children with disabilities are met.

9. **Legal Framework:** Government organizations provide a legal framework for the implementation of inclusive education policies and programs, such as the Persons with Disabilities Act and the Right to Education Act.

10. **Awareness and Communication:** Government organizations raise awareness about the importance of inclusive education and communicate with stakeholders about the policies and programs being implemented.

CHAPTER NINETEEN

Role of Non-Govt. Organizations in the Iimplementation of Inclusive Education

Non-government organizations (NGOs) play a vital role in supporting the implementation of inclusive education.

Some of the key roles of NGOs in inclusive education include:

1. **Advocacy:** NGOs advocate for the rights of children with disabilities and promote inclusive education policies and programs.
2. **Capacity Building:** NGOs provide training and capacity-building support to teachers, parents, and other stakeholders to enable them to effectively support inclusive education.
3. **Awareness Raising:** NGOs raise awareness about the importance of inclusive education and the rights of children with disabilities.
4. **Resource Mobilization:** NGOs mobilize resources to support inclusive education initiatives, such as funding for assistive technologies and teacher training.
5. **Service Provision:** NGOs provide direct services to children with disabilities, such as inclusive education programs and support services.
6. **Research and Knowledge Sharing:** NGOs conduct research on inclusive education to inform policy development and improve practice. They also share their knowledge and expertise with other stakeholders.
7. **Collaboration:** NGOs collaborate with other stakeholders, such as government organizations and disability organizations, to promote

inclusive education and improve outcomes for children with disabilities.

8. **Monitoring and Evaluation:** NGOs monitor and evaluate the implementation of inclusive education policies and programs to ensure that they are effective and meet the needs of all students.

9. **Networking:** NGOs create networks and alliances with other NGOs working in the field of inclusive education to share experiences and resources.

10. **Community Engagement:** NGOs engage with local communities to raise awareness about the importance of inclusive education and promote the inclusion of children with disabilities in community life.

CHAPTER TWENTY

Inclusive Education Models and Practices for Universal Schools (Class I to XII)

Here are 10 inclusive education models and practices for universal schools from Class I to XII:

1. **Universal Design for Learning (UDL):** UDL is an educational framework that provides multiple ways of representing information, multiple means of expression, and multiple ways of engagement to accommodate diverse learners.
2. **Response to Intervention (RTI):** RTI is a tiered approach to identify and support students with academic and behavioral challenges through a collaborative team-based problem-solving process.
3. **Co-teaching:** Co-teaching involves two or more teachers working together in the classroom to support all students, including those with disabilities.
4. **Differentiated instruction:** Differentiated instruction involves modifying teaching methods, content, and assessment to accommodate diverse learners.
5. **Peer-mediated instruction and support:** Peer-mediated instruction and support involves training and utilizing peers to provide academic and social support to students with disabilities.
6. **Collaborative teaming:** Collaborative teaming involves educators and other professionals working together to support the academic and social-emotional development of students with disabilities.

7. **Assistive technology:** Assistive technology refers to tools and devices that support learning and participation for students with disabilities, such as text-to-speech software, communication devices, and sensory tools.

8. **Universal Design for Assessment (UDA):** UDA involves designing assessments that are accessible to all students, including those with disabilities.

9. **Positive Behavioral Interventions and Supports (PBIS):** PBIS is a school-wide approach to promoting positive behavior and addressing challenging behavior through proactive and data-driven strategies.

10. **Inclusive extracurricular activities:** Inclusive extracurricular activities, such as sports, music, and drama, provide opportunities for all students to participate and develop their skills and talents, regardless of ability.

CHAPTER TWENTY-ONE

Universal Design for Learning (UDL)

Universal Design for Learning (UDL) is an educational framework that provides multiple means of representation, expression, and engagement to accommodate diverse learners. UDL is based on the principles of accessibility, flexibility, and equity, and aims to promote the success of all students, including those with disabilities.

Here are the three main principles of UDL:

1. **Multiple means of representation:** This principle involves presenting information in different ways to accommodate diverse learning styles and preferences. Examples of multiple means of representation include videos, images, diagrams, text-to-speech software, and closed captioning.
2. **Multiple means of expression:** This principle involves providing different ways for students to express their understanding and demonstrate their knowledge. Examples of multiple means of expression include writing, speaking, drawing, and using multimedia tools.
3. **Multiple means of engagement:** This principle involves providing opportunities for students to engage with the material in different ways, based on their interests, abilities, and backgrounds. Examples of multiple means of engagement include hands-on activities, group work, virtual simulations, and choice-based assignments.

Here are some examples of how UDL can be applied in the classroom:

1. Providing closed captioning on videos to accommodate students with hearing impairments.

2. Offering a range of reading materials, including text-to-speech software, audiobooks, and digital text, to accommodate students with visual impairments or reading difficulties.

3. Using a variety of teaching strategies, such as lectures, discussions, and multimedia presentations, to accommodate different learning styles.

4. Offering choice-based assignments, such as allowing students to choose between writing a paper, creating a video, or presenting a project, to accommodate different preferences and abilities.

5. Providing hands-on activities, such as science experiments, art projects, and field trips, to engage students with different learning styles and abilities.

UDL is a flexible and inclusive framework that can be applied across different subject areas, grade levels, and learning contexts. By using UDL principles, educators can create a learning environment that supports the success of all students, regardless of their abilities, backgrounds, or learning styles.

CHAPTER TWENTY-TWO

Individualized Education Program (IEP)

An Individualized Education Program (IEP) is a plan developed for students with disabilities to ensure that they receive the necessary accommodations and support to participate in the general education curriculum. Inclusive Education aims to ensure that students with disabilities are included in general education classrooms and have access to the same learning opportunities as their non-disabled peers. The IEP is a critical tool for achieving this goal.

Here is a detailed description of an IEP for Inclusive Education:

Evaluation and Identification: The first step in developing an IEP is to evaluate the student's needs and identify the specific disabilities that may be affecting their learning. This is usually done through formal assessments, observations, and consultations with parents, teachers, and other professionals.

Goal Setting: Based on the evaluation and identification, the IEP team sets measurable academic and functional goals for the student. These goals should be specific, measurable, achievable, relevant, and time-bound (SMART) and should align with the student's strengths, interests, and needs.

Accommodations and Modifications: The IEP team identifies the accommodations and modifications that will help the student achieve their goals and participate in the general education curriculum. Accommodations may include extra time on tests, access to assistive technology, or alternative formats for assignments. Modifications may include simplifying the curriculum or reducing the amount of work required.

Service Delivery: The IEP team determines the types and frequency of services that the student will receive to support their goals and accommodations. These services may include special education instruction, related services (such as speech therapy or occupational therapy), or support from paraprofessionals.

Progress Monitoring: The IEP team regularly monitors the student's progress toward their goals and makes adjustments to the plan as needed. Progress monitoring may include formal assessments, informal observations, and feedback from teachers and parents.

Transition Planning: For students who are approaching the end of their education or moving to a new school, the IEP team develops a transition plan to ensure that the student is prepared for the next phase of their life. This may include vocational training, college preparation, or independent living skills.

An IEP for Inclusive Education is a collaborative process involving parents, teachers, and other professionals. It is designed to ensure that students with disabilities have access to the same learning opportunities as their non-disabled peers and can achieve their full potential in the classroom and beyond.

CHAPTER TWENTY-THREE

Policy on Teachers for Children with Special Needs (CWSN)

In India, the policy on teachers for Children with Special Needs (CWSN) is guided by the provisions of the Right to Education Act, 2009, the National Policy on Education, 2020, and the Inclusive Education of Children with Disabilities Guidelines, 2018. The policy emphasizes the need to provide trained and qualified teachers to ensure that CWSN have access to quality education on an equal basis with other children.

Here are some key provisions of the policy on teachers for CWSN in India:

1. **Inclusive Teacher Education:** The policy emphasizes the need for pre-service and in-service teacher education programs to include inclusive education strategies and techniques to enable teachers to effectively cater to the diverse needs of CWSN.
2. **Qualified Teachers:** The policy mandates that all teachers working with CWSN should be qualified, trained, and certified in special education. The minimum qualification required is a diploma or certificate in special education.
3. **Special Educators:** The policy also recognizes the need for specialized teachers or special educators to support the educational needs of CWSN. These teachers should be trained and qualified in specific disabilities and should work in collaboration with general education teachers.
4. **Teacher Training and Support:** The policy emphasizes the need for ongoing training and support for teachers working with CWSN. This

includes professional development opportunities, access to resources, and mentoring and coaching programs.

5. **Inclusive Classroom Practices:** The policy encourages the use of inclusive classroom practices that promote participation, engagement, and learning for all students, including CWSN. This includes the use of assistive technology, accessible materials, and differentiated instruction.

6. **Parental Involvement:** The policy recognizes the important role of parents and caregivers in supporting the educational needs of CWSN. Teachers should work in partnership with parents to ensure that the needs of the child are met and that the child's educational goals are achieved.

7. **Monitoring and Evaluation:** The policy mandates regular monitoring and evaluation of teacher training programs and classroom practices to ensure that the needs of CWSN are being met and that quality education is being provided. This includes the use of assessment tools and feedback mechanisms to assess teacher performance and student learning outcomes.

The policy on teachers for CWSN emphasizes the need for a collaborative and inclusive approach to education that recognizes the diversity of learners and the unique needs of CWSN. It recognizes the importance of qualified and trained teachers and the need for ongoing support and professional development to ensure that CWSN have access to quality education on an equal basis with other children.

CHAPTER TWENTY-FOUR

Policy on Special Support Staff for CWSN

In India, the policy on special support staff for Children with Special Needs (CWSN) is guided by the provisions of the Right to Education Act, 2009, the National Policy on Education, 2020, and the Inclusive Education of Children with Disabilities Guidelines, 2018. The policy recognizes the importance of providing additional support and services to CWSN to ensure that they have access to quality education on an equal basis with other children.

Here are some key provisions of the policy on special support staff for CWSN in India:

1. **Identification and Assessment:** The policy emphasizes the need for a comprehensive assessment of the educational needs of CWSN to determine the type and level of support required. This includes the identification of special support staff needed to support the educational goals of CWSN.
2. **Support Staff Categories:** The policy recognizes the need for different categories of special support staff depending on the specific needs of CWSN. These may include sign language interpreters, braille writers, special educators, speech therapists, occupational therapists, and counselors, among others.
3. **Qualification and Training:** The policy mandates that all special support staff working with CWSN should be qualified, trained, and certified in their specific area of expertise. This includes ongoing professional development opportunities and access to resources and support.
4. **Inclusive Classroom Practices:** The policy emphasizes the need for special support staff to work in collaboration with general education teachers to ensure that inclusive classroom practices are being

implemented. This includes the use of assistive technology, accessible materials, and differentiated instruction.

5. **Parental Involvement:** The policy recognizes the important role of parents and caregivers in supporting the educational needs of CWSN. Special support staff should work in partnership with parents to ensure that the needs of the child are met and that the child's educational goals are achieved.

6. **Monitoring and Evaluation:** The policy mandates regular monitoring and evaluation of special support staff to ensure that the needs of CWSN are being met and that quality education is being provided. This includes the use of assessment tools and feedback mechanisms to assess staff performance and student learning outcomes.

The policy on special support staff for CWSN emphasizes the need for a collaborative and inclusive approach to education that recognizes the diversity of learners and the unique needs of CWSN. It recognizes the importance of qualified and trained support staff and the need for ongoing support and professional development to ensure that CWSN have access to quality education on an equal basis with other children.

CHAPTER TWENTY-FIVE

Physical Barriers in Universal Schooling

Here are 10 physical barriers that can prevent universal schooling in an inclusive setting:

1. **Inaccessible School Buildings**: School buildings that are not designed with accessibility in mind can pose physical barriers to students with disabilities. This includes buildings without ramps, elevators, accessible toilets, or adequate parking spaces for students with mobility impairments.
2. **Unsafe Infrastructure**: Schools with inadequate or poorly maintained infrastructure, such as unsafe staircases, broken floor tiles, or uneven surfaces can pose risks to students with mobility impairments.
3. **Inadequate Transportation**: Inadequate or inaccessible transportation can prevent students with disabilities from accessing schools. This includes inaccessible school buses or inadequate public transportation.
4. **Lack of Assistive Devices**: Students with disabilities require assistive devices such as hearing aids, wheelchairs, or braille readers to access education. However, the lack of such devices can prevent them from participating in school activities.
5. **Inadequate Lighting and Acoustics**: Inadequate lighting and acoustics can create barriers for students with visual and hearing impairments, respectively.
6. **Inadequate Restroom Facilities**: Inadequate or inaccessible restroom facilities can create barriers for students with disabilities, especially those with mobility impairments.
7. **Inaccessible Technology**: Technology plays an important role in the education of students with disabilities. However, inaccessible or non-

adaptive technology can pose a significant barrier to learning.

8. **Lack of Accessible Teaching Materials:** The lack of accessible teaching materials, such as textbooks in braille or large print, can prevent students with visual impairments from accessing education.

9. **Inaccessible Playgrounds:** Inaccessible or poorly designed playgrounds can prevent students with disabilities from participating in physical activities with their peers.

10. **Inadequate Sports Facilities:** Inadequate or inaccessible sports facilities can prevent students with disabilities from participating in physical education or sports activities.

Addressing physical barriers is an important step towards achieving inclusive education and ensuring that all students have access to quality education on an equal basis.

CHAPTER TWENTY-SIX

Social Barriers to Universal Schooling

Here are 10 social barriers that can prevent universal schooling in an inclusive setting:

1. **Stigma and Discrimination:** Students with disabilities may face stigma and discrimination from their peers, teachers, and the broader community, which can prevent them from accessing education.
2. **Lack of Awareness and Sensitivity:** The lack of awareness and sensitivity towards the needs of students with disabilities can prevent them from receiving appropriate support in school.
3. **Social Isolation:** Students with disabilities may feel socially isolated and excluded from their peers, which can prevent them from participating fully in school activities.
4. **Language Barriers:** Students who speak different languages or dialects may face barriers in accessing education, particularly if there are no provisions for teaching in their language.
5. **Limited Family Involvement:** The lack of involvement of families in their children's education can prevent students with disabilities from receiving the necessary support and advocacy.
6. **Lack of Accessibility in Public Spaces:** Inaccessible public spaces such as parks, playgrounds, and transportation can prevent students with disabilities from participating in extracurricular activities and attending school.
7. **Lack of Trained Teachers:** The lack of trained teachers with knowledge and skills in inclusive education can prevent students with disabilities from receiving the appropriate support in the classroom.

8. **Limited Resources:** Limited resources, including funding, personnel, and materials, can prevent schools from providing appropriate accommodations and support for students with disabilities.

9. **Limited Access to Technology:** Limited access to technology can prevent students with disabilities from accessing education materials and resources.

10. **Socioeconomic Status:** Students from low-income families may face social and economic barriers to accessing education, including lack of resources and support.

Addressing social barriers requires a concerted effort by all stakeholders, including teachers, families, community members, and policymakers, to create a supportive and inclusive environment for all students.

CHAPTER TWENTY-SEVEN

Economic Barriers to Universal Schooling

Here are 10 economic barriers that can prevent universal schooling in an inclusive setting:

1. **Poverty:** Children from economically disadvantaged families may face barriers in accessing education due to the lack of resources, including textbooks, school fees, uniforms, and transportation.
2. **Cost of Education:** The cost of education, including tuition fees, transportation, and school supplies, may be too high for families with limited financial resources.
3. **Child Labor:** Children from poor families may be forced to work to support their families, which can prevent them from attending school regularly.
4. **Lack of Infrastructure:** The lack of adequate infrastructure, including classrooms, toilets, and libraries, can prevent students from accessing quality education.
5. **Distance from School:** Children living in remote or rural areas may have to travel long distances to attend school, which can be a significant economic burden on families.
6. **Lack of Scholarships:** Limited access to scholarships and financial aid can prevent students from low-income families from attending school or accessing additional resources.
7. **Opportunity Cost:** Students from low-income families may have to forgo income-generating activities, such as working on farms or selling goods, to attend school, which can create an economic burden on their families.
8. **Inadequate Public Funding:** Inadequate public funding for education can limit the availability of resources and support for students with

disabilities or from low-income families.

9. **Limited Economic Opportunities:** Limited economic opportunities in certain areas can discourage families from investing in education and prevent students from accessing quality education.

10. **Unemployment:** The lack of employment opportunities for parents and caregivers can create economic barriers to education, particularly for children from low-income families.

To address economic barriers to universal schooling, governments, and policymakers need to develop and implement policies that prioritize education and provide support for families and students from disadvantaged backgrounds. This can include providing scholarships, funding schools in underserved areas, and creating economic opportunities for families.

Pedagogic Barriers to Universal Schooling

Here are 10 pedagogic barriers that can prevent universal schooling in an inclusive setting:

1. **Limited Access to Technology:** Students who lack access to technology, such as computers or the internet, may struggle to keep up with their peers and may not have the same educational opportunities.
2. **Inadequate Curriculum:** A curriculum that does not address the diverse learning needs of all students can prevent students from reaching their full potential.
3. **Limited Teacher Training:** Teachers who lack training in inclusive education may not have the necessary skills to teach children with diverse learning needs.
4. **Insufficient Teacher Support:** Teachers who lack support, such as mentorship or professional development opportunities, may struggle to provide inclusive education to all students.
5. **High Student-to-Teacher Ratios:** Large class sizes can make it difficult for teachers to provide individualized attention to each student, particularly those with special needs.
6. **Traditional Teaching Methods:** Traditional teaching methods that rely heavily on lectures and rote memorization may not be effective for all students, particularly those with diverse learning needs.
7. **Limited Use of Multisensory Learning:** Students who learn through different modalities, such as visual or kinesthetic, may struggle if lessons do not incorporate multisensory learning.
8. **Insufficient Adaptations:** Lack of adaptations to the learning environment, such as classroom design or teaching materials, can create

barriers for students with diverse needs.

9. **Negative Attitudes:** Negative attitudes towards students with disabilities or those from different cultural backgrounds can create a hostile learning environment and prevent students from fully participating in the classroom.

10. **Limited Parent and Community Engagement:** Lack of engagement from parents and the community can make it difficult to create a supportive learning environment for all students.

To address these pedagogic barriers, schools and teachers need to adopt inclusive teaching methods that address the diverse learning needs of all students. This can include using technology to support learning, providing teachers with training and support, and creating a supportive learning environment that engages parents and the community.

CHAPTER TWENTY-NINE

Provisions for Children with Special Needs (CWSN) in India

Here are 15 provisions for children with special needs (CWSN) in different education initiatives in India:

1. **Sarva Shiksha Abhiyan (SSA):** SSA aims to provide universal access to education for all children, including CWSN. It provides for the identification, assessment, and appropriate educational interventions for CWSN, including the provision of special teachers, aids, and appliances.
2. **Rashtriya Madhyamik Shiksha Abhiyan (RMSA):** RMSA aims to provide access to quality secondary education for all, including CWSN. It provides for the identification, assessment, and provision of appropriate educational interventions for CWSN.
3. **Integrated Child Development Services (ICDS):** ICDS provides for the identification, assessment, and referral of children with special needs to appropriate services, including educational services.
4. **Inclusive Education for Disabled at Secondary Stage (IEDSS):** IEDSS provides for the education of CWSN in regular schools, with the provision of necessary support, aids, and appliances.
5. **National Programme for Education of Girls at Elementary Level (NPEGEL):** NPEGEL provides for the education of girls, including those with disabilities, at the elementary level.
6. **Mid-day Meal Scheme:** The Mid-day Meal Scheme provides for the provision of a hot, cooked meal to children in government schools, including CWSN.

7. **Right to Education (RTE) Act:** The RTE Act provides for free and compulsory education for all children aged 6 to 14, including CWSN. It provides for the identification and assessment of CWSN and the provision of appropriate educational interventions.

8. **National Curriculum Framework (NCF):** The NCF provides guidelines for the development of a curriculum that is inclusive of CWSN.

9. **National Policy on Education (NPE):** The NPE provides guidelines for the education of all children, including CWSN, with the aim of creating an inclusive and equitable education system.

10. **National Skill Development Corporation (NSDC):** The NSDC provides training and skill development opportunities for CWSN to help them achieve their full potential.

11. **Inclusive Education for the Visually Challenged (IEVC):** IEVC provides for the education of visually challenged children in regular schools, with the provision of necessary support, aids, and appliances.

12. **Inclusive Education for the Hearing Impaired (IEHI):** IEHI provides for the education of hearing-impaired children in regular schools, with the provision of necessary support, aids, and appliances.

13. **National Institute of Open Schooling (NIOS):** NIOS provides opportunities for CWSN to complete their education through open and distance learning.

14. **Vocational Education:** Vocational education programmes provide opportunities for CWSN to acquire vocational skills and become self-reliant.

15. **Scholarships and Financial Assistance:** Various scholarships and financial assistance schemes are available to support the education of CWSN, including the National Scholarship for Persons with Disabilities and the Rajiv Gandhi National Fellowship for Students with Disabilities.

The Inclusive Education for Disabled at Secondary Stage (IEDSS)

The Inclusive Education for Disabled at Secondary Stage (IEDSS) is a government initiative in India that aims to provide support to children with disabilities in secondary schools. It was launched in 2009 and is implemented in partnership with the state governments.

The key features of IEDSS include:

1. **Identification and assessment of children with disabilities:** The initiative provides for the identification and assessment of children with disabilities in secondary schools through a comprehensive screening process.

2. **Provision of aids and appliances:** IEDSS provides for the provision of aids and appliances such as hearing aids, wheelchairs, and Braille books to students with disabilities.

3. **Support for teachers:** The initiative provides for training and support for teachers in inclusive education practices, as well as the appointment of resource teachers to support children with disabilities.

4. **Curriculum adaptation:** IEDSS provides for the adaptation of the curriculum to meet the needs of children with disabilities. This includes providing access to textbooks in accessible formats such as Braille and audio, as well as adapting teaching methods and assessment procedures.

5. **Accessibility of infrastructure:** IEDSS provides for the provision of accessible infrastructure such as ramps, accessible toilets, and other facilities to ensure that children with disabilities have equal access to

education.

6. **Vocational training and career guidance:** The initiative provides vocational training and career guidance to students with disabilities to enhance their employability and independence.

7. **Collaboration with NGOs:** IEDSS encourages collaboration with NGOs and other stakeholders to support the education of children with disabilities.

8. **Financial assistance:** IEDSS provides financial assistance to schools to support the education of children with disabilities. This includes funds for aids and appliances, infrastructure development, and teacher training.

Examples of how IEDSS has been implemented include:

1. The provision of assistive devices such as hearing aids and Braille books to students with disabilities.

2. The adaptation of the curriculum to meet the needs of students with disabilities. For example, providing textbooks in accessible formats and adapting teaching methods.

3. The training of teachers in inclusive education practices, and the appointment of resource teachers to support students with disabilities.

4. The provision of accessible infrastructure such as ramps and accessible toilets.

5. The provision of vocational training and career guidance to enhance the employability and independence of students with disabilities.

6. Collaboration with NGOs and other stakeholders to support the education of children with disabilities.

IEDSS is an important initiative that has helped to improve the education outcomes of children with disabilities in India. By providing support for identification, assessment, infrastructure development, and teacher training, IEDSS has helped to ensure that children with disabilities have access to quality education and the opportunity to develop their full potential.

Inclusive Education for Disabled at Secondary Stage (IEDSS) is a centrally sponsored scheme by the Ministry of Education, Government of

India, which aims to provide educational opportunities to children with disabilities in the age group of 14 to 18 years. The scheme is implemented in all government and government-aided schools across India.

Pedagogy in IEDSS:

- IEDSS emphasizes the use of multi-sensory teaching methods and technologies to provide an inclusive learning environment for children with disabilities.
- Teachers are trained to use Universal Design for Learning (UDL) principles, which involve designing instruction that is accessible and effective for all learners, regardless of their ability level.
- The focus is on providing personalized and flexible learning experiences to cater to the diverse needs of students with disabilities.

Curriculum in IEDSS:

- The curriculum is based on the National Curriculum Framework (NCF) and the syllabus is adapted to meet the specific needs of students with disabilities.
- The emphasis is on providing practical, hands-on learning experiences to help students acquire practical skills that can be used in their daily lives.
- The curriculum is designed to promote functional literacy, numeracy, communication skills, and social skills.

Assessment of Learning Outcomes in IEDSS:

- The scheme emphasizes continuous and comprehensive evaluation (CCE) to assess the learning outcomes of students with disabilities.
- The assessment is based on the principles of formative and summative evaluation and is conducted through a variety of tools and techniques, such as observation, portfolios, and project work.

- The focus is on providing feedback that is specific, constructive, and actionable to help students improve their learning outcomes.

In summary, IEDSS provides a comprehensive framework for inclusive education for students with disabilities at the secondary stage. The scheme focuses on providing a multi-sensory, personalized, and flexible learning environment that is adapted to meet the specific needs of students with disabilities. The curriculum is designed to promote functional skills, while the assessment is based on continuous and comprehensive evaluation to provide specific feedback that can help students improve their learning outcomes.

Rashtriya Madhyamik Shiksha Abhiyan (RMSA)

Rashtriya Madhyamik Shiksha Abhiyan (RMSA) is a centrally sponsored scheme launched in 2009 with the aim of improving access, equity, and quality of education at the secondary level. The scheme covers all government secondary schools and aims to provide universal access to secondary education by 2020.

Objectives of RMSA:

- To improve access to secondary education, particularly for girls, SCs, STs, and other marginalized groups
- To improve the quality of education through the implementation of a teacher training program, curriculum reform, and the provision of better facilities and infrastructure
- To promote skill development among students to make them employable
- To enhance the educational opportunities in backward areas by opening new schools or upgrading existing ones

Some of the key features of RMSA are:

- Infrastructure development: The scheme provides funding for the construction of new schools, upgrading existing schools, and provision of necessary facilities like laboratories, libraries, and computer rooms.

- Quality improvement: The scheme focuses on improving the quality of education through the development of a teacher training program, curriculum reform, and the provision of better teaching and learning materials.
- Skill development: RMSA aims to promote skill development among students to make them employable by providing vocational education and training.
- Inclusive education: The scheme aims to provide education to all, with a special focus on the education of girls, SCs, STs, and other marginalized groups.

Examples of RMSA implementation:

- In the state of Assam, the RMSA has been successful in increasing the enrollment of students in secondary schools. As a result, the number of secondary schools has increased, and the state has been able to provide education to a larger number of students.
- In Jharkhand, RMSA has helped to provide necessary infrastructure and facilities to schools in rural areas, including the construction of new classrooms, laboratories, and libraries. The scheme has also provided training to teachers and supported the development of a new curriculum.
- In Odisha, the RMSA has focused on improving the quality of education by providing teacher training and introducing innovative teaching methods. The scheme has also helped to improve the infrastructure of schools, including the provision of better facilities for sports and extracurricular activities.

Pedagogy:

The RMSA emphasizes the need to ensure that students receive a high-quality education that is relevant to their needs and prepares them for higher education and the workforce. The scheme seeks to promote an inclusive learning environment and provides support for the development of a learner-centered pedagogy that focuses on active learning and critical thinking. To this end, the RMSA provides funds for the development of teaching-learning materials and teacher training programs.

Curriculum:

The RMSA supports the development of a flexible curriculum that is responsive to the diverse needs of students. The scheme recognizes the importance of providing a broad and balanced education that includes academic, vocational, and life skills. The RMSA provides funds for the development of curriculum frameworks and teaching-learning materials that are relevant to the local context and meet the needs of all learners, including those with disabilities.

Assessment of learning outcomes:

The RMSA recognizes the importance of measuring learning outcomes and uses a variety of assessment tools to evaluate student achievement. The scheme provides funds for the development of assessment frameworks and tools that are aligned with the curriculum and support the development of key competencies. The RMSA also provides support for the development of a system for monitoring and evaluating the quality of education at the secondary level.

In summary, the RMSA focuses on improving access, equity, and quality of education at the secondary level by promoting an inclusive learning environment, providing support for the development of learner-centered pedagogy, promoting a flexible and relevant curriculum, and using a variety of assessment tools to evaluate student achievement.

CHAPTER THIRTY-TWO

Social Welfare Schemes for Gender, Marginalized and Disabled groups

There are various social welfare schemes launched by the Government of India for the upliftment of gender, marginalized, and disabled groups.
Here are some examples:

1. **Beti Bachao, Beti Padhao Yojana:** This scheme aims to improve the status of the girl child and promote her education. The scheme provides financial assistance for the education of girls and focuses on their welfare and empowerment.

2. **National Rural Livelihoods Mission (NRLM):** This scheme focuses on the empowerment of rural women through the creation of self-help groups, skill development, and entrepreneurship.

3. **National Scholarship Scheme for Persons with Disabilities:** This scheme provides financial assistance to students with disabilities for their education. The scheme covers tuition fees, books, and other expenses related to education.

4. **Swadhar Greh Scheme:** This scheme provides shelter, food, and other facilities to women in difficult circumstances, including widows, destitute women, and women rescued from trafficking.

5. **National Food Security Act:** This scheme aims to provide food security to vulnerable and marginalized sections of society by providing subsidized food grains through the public distribution system.

6. **National Health Insurance Scheme (Ayushman Bharat):** This scheme provides free healthcare services to economically weaker sections of

society, including women, marginalized groups, and persons with disabilities.

7. **Accessible India Campaign:** This scheme aims to make public places and transport systems accessible to persons with disabilities by providing barrier-free access.

8. **Integrated Child Development Services (ICDS):** This scheme provides nutrition, healthcare, and education services to children under the age of six and their mothers from marginalized communities.

9. **National Scheme of Incentives to Girls for Secondary Education:** This scheme provides financial incentives to girls from marginalized communities to encourage them to complete their secondary education.

10. **Pradhan Mantri Awas Yojana:** This scheme provides affordable housing to economically weaker sections of society, including women and marginalized groups.

11. **National Urban Livelihoods Mission (NULM):** This scheme focuses on the empowerment of urban poor women by providing them with skill development and entrepreneurship opportunities.

12. **Rashtriya Swasthya Bima Yojana:** This scheme provides health insurance to workers in the unorganized sector, including women and persons with disabilities.

13. **Sukanya Samriddhi Yojana:** This scheme is aimed at promoting the welfare of the girl child by providing financial security for her education and marriage.

14. **Deen Dayal Disabled Rehabilitation Scheme:** This scheme provides financial assistance for the education, training, and rehabilitation of persons with disabilities.

15. **Pradhan Mantri Matru Vandana Yojana:** This scheme provides financial assistance to pregnant and lactating women from marginalized communities for their health and nutrition needs.

CHAPTER THIRTY-THREE

Evaluation and Analysis of Social Welfare schemes

Evaluation and analysis of social welfare schemes for gender, marginalized, and disabled groups are critical to ensure that the intended beneficiaries are receiving the intended benefits.

Here are some key factors to consider when evaluating and analyzing social welfare schemes for these groups:

1. **Accessibility:** The schemes should be accessible to the targeted group. For instance, if the scheme is meant for disabled individuals, it should be designed in a way that accommodates their needs.
2. **Affordability:** The cost of the scheme should be reasonable, and the targeted group should be able to afford it. In cases where the scheme involves a fee, it should be affordable for those who need it the most.
3. **Impact:** The scheme's effectiveness in achieving its objectives should be assessed regularly. For example, a scheme meant to empower women financially should be evaluated on whether it has contributed to improving their economic status.
4. **Inclusivity:** The scheme should not exclude any group within the targeted population. For instance, if the scheme is for women, it should be accessible to women from all ethnic, racial, and socio-economic backgrounds.
5. **Participation:** The targeted group should be involved in the design, implementation, and monitoring of the scheme. Their feedback can be used to improve the scheme and ensure it meets their needs.
6. **Sustainability:** The scheme should be sustainable in the long run. For example, if the scheme is dependent on external funding, measures should be taken to ensure that it remains viable even after the funding

ends.

7. **Efficiency:** The scheme should be efficiently managed to minimize waste and maximize impact. For example, resources should be allocated efficiently, and bureaucratic procedures should be streamlined.

8. **Transparency:** The scheme's management and operations should be transparent, and beneficiaries should be aware of their entitlements and the process for claiming them.

9. **Coordination:** Coordination between different agencies and departments responsible for implementing social welfare schemes for gender, marginalized, and disabled groups is critical. This coordination ensures that the schemes are complementary and not duplicative.

In conclusion, evaluation and analysis of social welfare schemes for gender, marginalized, and disabled groups are essential to ensure that the schemes are effective, efficient, and equitable. It is also critical to involve the targeted group in the design, implementation, and monitoring of the scheme to ensure it meets their needs.

CHAPTER THIRTY-FOUR

Highs and Lows of Social Welfare Schemes for Gender, Marginalized, and Disabled groups

Here are 10 highs and lows of social welfare schemes for gender, marginalized, and disabled groups:

Highs:

1. **Increased access to education:** Social welfare schemes have helped increase access to education for girls, persons with disabilities, and marginalized communities, which can lead to improved social and economic outcomes.
2. **Improved healthcare:** Social welfare schemes provide free or subsidized healthcare to vulnerable sections of society, which can help improve health outcomes and reduce healthcare costs.
3. **Increased financial inclusion:** Many social welfare schemes provide financial assistance to marginalized communities, helping them become financially self-sufficient and reducing their dependence on others.
4. **Improved infrastructure:** Social welfare schemes have helped improve infrastructure, such as roads, water supply, and sanitation facilities, which can improve the quality of life of marginalized communities.
5. **Increased social awareness:** Social welfare schemes have helped raise awareness about the rights and needs of marginalized communities and

have helped reduce discrimination against them.

Lows:

1. **Inadequate implementation:** Many social welfare schemes suffer from inadequate implementation, which can result in a lack of benefits reaching the intended beneficiaries.
2. **Corruption and fraud:** Corruption and fraud are prevalent in some social welfare schemes, resulting in the misuse of funds and benefits intended for vulnerable communities.
3. **Insufficient funding:** Many social welfare schemes suffer from insufficient funding, which can limit their effectiveness and impact.
4. **Lack of participation:** Some social welfare schemes suffer from low participation rates among vulnerable communities, resulting in a lack of benefits reaching those who need them the most.
5. **Lack of accountability:** Some social welfare schemes suffer from a lack of accountability, making it difficult to identify and address implementation issues and improve the impact of the schemes.

CHAPTER THIRTY-FIVE

Quotes on Inclusion

- "Inclusion is not a strategy to help people fit into the systems and structures which exist in our societies; it is about transforming those systems and structures to make it better for everyone." - Diane Richler
- "The one who is different from us is the one who will teach us the most." - Paulo Coelho
- "Diversity is being invited to the party. Inclusion is being asked to dance." - Verna Myers
- "Inclusion is a state of mind that says everyone is valued, everyone has a place, and everyone deserves respect." - Mark E. Smith
- "We are all different, which is great because we are all unique. Without diversity life would be very boring." - Catherine Pulsifer
- "The only way to do great work is to love what you do. If you haven't found it yet, keep looking. Don't settle. As with all matters of the heart, you'll know when you find it." - Steve Jobs
- "Inclusion is about creating an environment where everyone feels valued and respected." - Mary-Frances Winters
- "The best way to predict your future is to create it." - Abraham Lincoln
- "If you have come to help me, you are wasting your time. But if you have come because your liberation is bound up with mine, then let us work together." - Lilla Watson
- "The function of education is to teach one to think intensively and to think critically. Intelligence plus character - that is the goal of true education." - Martin Luther King Jr.

End Note

As we come to the end of this book on inclusive education at the secondary stage, it is my hope that it has provided valuable insights and practical strategies for educators, parents, and policymakers who are committed to creating a more inclusive and equitable education system.

Inclusive education is not just about meeting the needs of students with disabilities or special needs, but it is about ensuring that every student feels valued, respected, and supported in their learning journey. By embracing diversity, promoting empathy, and providing a safe and inclusive learning environment, we can help students develop the skills and knowledge they need to succeed in life.

As educators, we have a responsibility to ensure that every student has access to quality education, regardless of their background or abilities. This book has been written with that goal in mind, and I hope that it will inspire and empower educators to take action and make a positive difference in the lives of their students.

In conclusion, I would like to thank all those who have contributed to this book and those who have supported the cause of inclusive education. Let us continue to work together towards a more inclusive and equitable education system, where every student has the opportunity to reach their full potential.